Pocketguide to

Gangs

and their Symbols:

Street Gangs, Ethnic Gangs, Occult Groups,
Prison Gangs, Outlaw Motorcycle Gangs,
Hate Groups, Extremists, Terrorists

by
Louis A. Savelli

D1714894

43-08 162nd Street
Flushing, NY 11358
800-647-5547
www.LooseleafLaw.com

ISBN-10:   1-889031-96-8

ISBN-13:   978-1-889031-96-5

Cover design by *Sans Serif, Inc.* Saline, Michigan

About the Pocketguide Series

Law Enforcement Officers (LEOs) are faced with ever-changing trends and issues and have little time to spend on in-depth research and reference. The Pocketguide series of books have been created to assist law enforcement officers in the endeavor to remain up-to-date on these ever-changing trends. The Pocketguide series provides to the point reference information on contemporary important issues. We at Homefront Protective Group, creators of the Pocketguide series, have painstakingly researched and developed the following valuable and useful information.

The Pocketguide books, as you will see, will provide a current, quick and easy-to- use, pocket-sized tool that was written in an easy to read style. When hundreds of pages of information or volumes of material are not feasible to carry around and time does not permit its study, the Pocketguide books will fill that void and provide the right reference.

Please enjoy this useful pocket-sized book and keep in mind that we wish you safety and efficiency in your endeavor to fight the scourge of crime in our society.

Other Pocketguides now available:

Identity Theft
Basic Crime Scene Investigation
*A Proactive Law Enforcement Guide for
    the War on Terror*
Street Drugs Identification
Graffiti
The Best Cops Jokes Ever
E-Z Spanish for Police

Request a *free* complete catalog
Toll-Free (800) 647-5547
or online www.LooseleafLaw.com

Looseleaf Law Publications, Inc.
Flushing, NY

About the Author

Lou Savelli, who has spent **all** of his 25 years in law enforcement in the streets, is one of the most decorated officers in NYPD history. He has received over 100 medals for bravery, outstanding police work, life saving rescues, and record-setting investigations. He was chosen as one of the **top 10 of NYPD's most effective leaders of all ranks** (out of nearly 20,000 qualified supervisors in NYPD) and the first supervisor featured in NYPD's Leadership Training School Newsletter because of his innovation and success in the field of leadership and policing.

He created NYPD's first citywide gang unit called CAGE (Citywide Anti Gang Enforcement) which was awarded the National Gang Crime Research Center's award for **The Most Effective Gang Unit in the US**. He has received awards from the FBI, DEA, ATF, Dept of Treasury, US Attorney's Office, Department of State, Los Angeles Sheriff's Department, Canadian law enforcement agencies, Caribbean Law Enforcement Agencies, Italian Government, New South Wales Australia, New Zealand, Mexico, Japan, and many other law enforcement agencies, government agencies and community groups. As a detective, he and his unit were responsible for the **World's Largest Cash Seizure in a Drug Case** ($20 Million) which still holds as a record to this date.

While much of Lou Savelli's investigations are still confidential, he is an internationally-sought after trainer on gangs, youth at risk, terrorism, narcotics investigations, street tactics, drug smuggling, and crime fighting. He has personally lectured before countless audiences, in law enforcement and the private sector, in three countries. He has been frequently quoted in major periodicals such as the *LA Times*, *New York Times*, *New York Newsday*, *New York Daily News*, *Nottingham Press* (United Kingdom), television news reports, many local newspapers across the US and has had his investigations featured in **Time Magazine**, **Newsweek**, **Top Cops TV Series**, **Law Enforcement Technology Magazine**, **American Police Beat Magazine** and other periodicals. Lou Savelli has consulted on such television shows as **Third Watch** (NBC) and *One Life to Live* (ABC) and provided intricate authentic information to television shows such as New York Undercover. He can be seen on the Good Life Network in the documentary series **Homefront America** which examines Homeland Security in the United States today.

As the author of five law enforcement books, several true crime short stories, and numerous articles relating to issues such as terrorism, gangs, criminal investigation, identity theft, and crime prevention, Lou Savelli is a frequent consultant to hundreds of law enforcement officers, throughout the United States and abroad, seeking advice on how to successfully identify and fight crime in their own cities. Lou Savelli has worked extensively with youth at risk, gang members and has conducted educational and motivational speeches for counselors involved in youth and drug counseling.

Lou Savelli is the cofounder and Deputy Director of the East Coast Gang Investigators Assn, a member of the International Counter Terrorism Officers Assn, Midwest Gang Investigators Assn, Oklahoma Gang Investigators Assn, Florida Gang Investigators Assn, International Latino Gang Investigators Assn, International Outlaw Motorcycle Gang Investigators Assn, California Gang Investigators Association, Ontario National Gang Investigators Assn, Southeast Connecticut Gang Activities Group, GANGINFO Network, National Assn of Bunco Investigators, International Association of Identification, Roadwarrior Interdiction Network, and several others. He is a long standing member of several fraternal and law enforcement support associations such as National Police Defense Foundation, Fraternal Order of Police, and International Police Association. Lou Savelli currently holds membership in law enforcement and security professional associations, to wit: International Association of Chiefs of Police (IACP), American Academy for Professional Law Enforcement (AAPLE), and American Society of Industrial Security (ASIS).

His carefully chosen law enforcement instructors provide several training courses each year for the Northeast Counterdrug Training Center, Midwest Counterdrug Training Center, Regional Counterdrug Training Center, RISS Networks, and many other training academies throughout the United States. Lou Savelli and his instructors have been extremely successful in providing state of the art 'Reality' training to small and rural agencies, as well as larger law enforcement agencies.

He recently retired as the Detective Squad Commander of the NYPD Terrorism Interdiction Unit, which is a pro-active counter-terrorism unit aggressively targeting al-Qaeda and other foreign terrorist groups in the United States. He is a veteran of the rescue and recovery effort at the World Trade Center resulting from the attacks on 9-11-01.

Lou Savelli is an active member of the International Law Enforcement Educators and Trainers Association (ILEETA) and American Society of Law Enforcement Trainers (ASLET) and is President of Homefront Protective Group, a law enforcement training company. He can be reached at the company's website: www.homefront protect.com.

Table of Contents

Introduction

The *Pocketguide* **to Gangs and their Symbols** has been compiled from a variety of sources. It is meant to be a convenient 'pocket' reference on most gangs/groups encountered today. These gangs/groups are spreading rapidly. The gangs highlighted in this pocketguide can be found in many countries across the world and are not limited to North America. We need to identify their signs and symbols before they become entrenched in our own communities. This Pocketguide is the best tool available to identify these signs at any time. In this second edition, a multitude of symbols, phrases, words and numbers have been added. This Pocketguide is a handy reference book that can be carried around daily to help identify the signs and symbols of gangs, anywhere. Each section is useful in identifying and dealing with gangs and related groups. *Analyzing Gang Graffiti,* will teach you to identify the signs of gang violence and potential trouble. *How to Identify if someone is in a gang* will increase your awareness to the characteristics of people in a gang. Use the sections on G*ang Symbols* to familiarize yourself and your community with the most common signs of gangs. The *Color Guide* will increase your awareness to the colors used to represent these gangs in their everyday dress and graffiti.

A new section has been added to identify sports apparel and designer clothing worn by gangs. The Pocketguide has a **Symbol Reference** of several hundreds of symbols, phrases, words, and numbers, along with their meanings and the gang to which they are associated.

The History of Gangs

An American Perspective

Gangs have been in existence for as long as there have been inhabitants of this world. The word thug dates back to India between the years 600 to 1200 AD and it refers to a gang of criminals (***Thugz or Thugee Cult***) that roamed the country pillaging towns in their course. These ***Thugz*** had its own symbols, hand signs, rituals and slang. In the United States, we grew up with tales of our own form of thugs like pirates and gangsters, therefore, gangs, undoubtedly, are not a new concept.

Throughout the 1800's, Americans were fascinated with gangs and gangsters. The **James Gang**, **Billy the Kid** and other outlaws, legend has it, ruled the Wild West. As the late 1800's roared in, the new generation of gangs and gangsters was created out of the new immigrants. Irish gangs like the **Whyos**, **Dead Rabbits** and **Plug Uglies,** and Jewish gangs like the **Monk Eastman Gang** terrorized New York City streets. The most notorious gang during this era formed in New York City during the late 1890's and early 1900's. This gang, called the **Five Points Gang,** because of its home turf being situated in the Five Points (Bowery) Section of Lower

Manhattan, would change the mold of the American outlaw forever.

The Five Points Gang, led by Italian immigrant, Paolo Antonini Vaccarelli, also known as Paul Kelly and his second in command, Johnny Torrio, was the most significant street gang to form in the United States, ever! Johnny Torrio, who became a significant member of the Sicilian Mafia (La Cosa Nostra), recruited street hoodlums from across New York City to the Five Points Gang. The Five Points Gang became the Major League to many young street gangsters and a farm club for the Mafia. The most notorious recruit into the Five Points Gang was a teenaged boy of Italian descent who was born in Williamsburg, Brooklyn in 1899 to immigrant parents. His name was Alphonse Capone, better known as Scarface. He became a member of the James Street Gang, which was a minor league of sort, to the Five Pointers. One of Capone's childhood friends, and fellow member of the Five Points Gang, was another street thug named Lucky Luciano.

In 1919, while being sought by authorities in connection with a gangland murder in New

York, Al "Scarface" Capone moved to Chicago when summoned by Johnny Torrio. Torrio needed his assistance in maintaining control of Chicago mob territories. Al Capone, eventually became the most violent and prolific gangster in Chicago, if not, the United States, law enforcement has ever experienced. The Al Capone style of gangster has molded the American gangster experience. As will be illustrated later, it is alive today in our street gangs from a variety of backgrounds and races.

As street gangs, influenced by mobsters such as Capone, flourished during the 1920's and 30's gangs became a symbol of lower income neighborhoods and ethnic ghettos. America's new immigrant communities and ghetto neighborhoods saw their youth forming gangs. African Americans, Asians and Hispanics made up the majority of street gangs that sociologists would research but the majority of all communities were experiencing street gangs in some degree. During the early 1940's, Mexican gangs formed along the west coast of the United States. As the late 1940's and 50's came along, gangs like the Latin Kings and Vice Lords were formed in Chicago, Illinois.

With civil strife and disenchantment abound during the 1960's, African American street gangs formed in large urban cities such as Chicago, Los Angeles and New York.

New York street gangs formed under names like the **Savage Skulls**, **La Familia** and **Savage Nomads**. Another New York Street gang during this time known as the **Rampers** has recently realized the infamy of one its members who is contemporarily known as Sammy *"the Bull"* Gravano. By the late 1960's and early 1970's, **Crips** gangs in Los Angeles were so violent and entrenched in ghetto neighborhoods that rival **Bloods** gangs formed to challenge the strength of the Crips. Meanwhile, Chicago experienced the creation of the **Black Gangsters**, **Devil's Disciples** and **Black P Stone Rangers**, to name a few. The late 1970's and early 1980's paved the way for creation of national gang alliances, expansion of national drug networks and the glorification of gangsters with movies like Colors and Scarface.

By the late 1980's and early 1990's, drug networks were in full swing. Drug importation from Southeast Asia and Colombia were at its peak. The United States becomes known as the number one drug consumer in the world. Street gangs develop into drug gangs with businesslike operations. Violence becomes standard operating procedure for these gangs. During this time, gangs are spreading like wildfire. **Super Gangs,** like the **Latin Kings**, **Bloods**, **Crips, 18th Street** and **Gangster Disciples** have spread their influence across North America. Major cities were suffering from the violence connected to these gangs.

During the mid 1990's, crime rates begin to plummet across the nation. Despite the decrease in crime, street gangs were forming at a high rate. Each year, the number of gangs and gang members reported in surveys increased. Major cities across the United States begin the develop strategies to combat gangs within their boundaries. Ironically, statistics show the suburban gang situation to have the greatest increase. By the late 1990's, the previously mentioned Super Gangs (large, multi-cultural/multi-state, violent, drug oriented street gangs) became well-entrenched in many North American communities despite the steadily falling crime rate. In the year 2002, street gangs were estimated to show a membership of nearly one million members and some experts believe that number will exceed one million by the year 2004. During 2003, gangsters have reached a new level of sophistication and have forged alliances with other criminal enterprises to create a stronger power base but the efforts of the modern gang investigator has, and will, undoubtedly, hinder their efforts!

Gangs relate to their own glorification in the many gangster rap songs, magazines and videos flooding the media. This has given them fame rather than infamy. It is

7

apparent in today's clothing and language of our youth how much street gangs have influenced our culture. Emulation of the old gangsters, their names, colloquialisms and their practices are being acted out in the streets of our cities and towns. Gang members are referring to themselves as ***made men*** and have monikers of ***John Gotti*** or ***Al Capone***. Modern gangsters are studying the ways of past gangsters and readying themselves for the future. With all this momentum, we, as a society and a community, must be ready. The following pages is a start!

Understanding and Analyzing Gang Graffiti

The key to understanding gang graffiti is being able to analyze the symbols, indicators and terminology used by gangs. Simply, gangs use graffiti to send messages. The purpose of these messages is:

- ✓ to mark the gang's turf (territory)
- ✓ to disrespect a rival gang or gang member
- ✓ to memorialize a deceased gang member
- ✓ to make a statement
- ✓ to send a message
- ✓ to conduct business.

Gangs mark their turf by 'tagging' conspicuous walls and surfaces to let other gangs know this turf is 'claimed.' A tag simply stating "Nine Trey Gangsters" or just 'NTG' indicates to rival gangs that the Nine Trey Gangster Bloods have claimed this neighborhood as their turf. Occasionally gang members will write the street name or neighborhood in the tag.

When a gangster wants to disrespect a rival gang, he/she will tag (write) over his/her rival's graffiti or personal tag. This is an overt sign of disrespect. Other signs of disrespect are writing the name or symbol of a rival gang upside down or on its side, crossing out the rival's tag, or placing a line through a letter that represents the rival gang. In the depiction of typical gang graffiti above, Crips tagged on a wall on 'Blood' turf which is marked with *"Bloods Rule."* Notice the '*B*'s' are crossed out and the word *slob* is used as a derogatory name for Bloods. *Slob Killas* is another name for Crips since Crips consider themselves killers of

Bloods. BK is commonly used by Crips and it stands for **Blood Killer.**

To memorialize a fallen member of the gang, gangsters will go to great lengths to create elaborate murals. They will even go to greater lengths to protect their work and the memory of the lost *homie*. Such "*In memory of*" and "*Rest in Peace*" murals are very difficult to create but when completed are usually extremely artistic. Most of the members of the gang, if not all, will want to 'tag' their names on the mural as a sign of respect as well as way of gaining fame. Such elaborate murals become advertising for the gang and create a sense of stature.

In the following picture, the gang painted a colorful Rest in Peace mural to Alex. Gang members will inscribe

their names on the mural to pay respect to the dead gangsters and receive '***props***' for having their name seen on such an eye-catching mural.

To make a statement, gang graffiti is quite straightforward and less artistic. Gang members will write concise short statements in their graffiti to send a strong message. Statements like, "***Crips must die***," is a straightforward statement of the gang's intentions. Many times the gang will use violence indicators such as **187** (California Penal Code number for Murder), **T.O.S.** (Terminate On Sight) or draw a picture of 'Crosshairs' (**target sights** *as seen below*) over a rival gangster's name. This indicates the intention of shooting the rival or ordering his death.

Gangs conduct business through graffiti by writing trademarks of drugs sold or showing where to buy their drugs. In the following picture, a gang simply wrote ***Chronic,*** which means Marijuana and painted an arrow to the building in which they were selling. Street people will know where to go to by reading the signs of graffiti and following its instructions. There are many other ways to conduct business through graffiti besides the way it is illustrated in the following picture.

There are other ways gangs conduct business by the use of graffiti:

✓ The use of colors to indicate the color or colors of the packaging of the drugs being sold at a particular street corner

- ✓ Tagging a trademark, symbol, or stamp on a wall to indicate the "brand name" of the drugs being sold at a local drug den
- ✓ Writing the seller's nickname in graffiti to alert the drug users who is slinging (selling). An example of the nickname, "NATE" of the drug dealer on a wall used for passing messages about drugs is pictured here:

Graffiti is considered the newspaper of the streets and it is undoubtedly full of information. Graffiti is usually the first indication that there is a gang presence in a neighborhood as well as a good indicator that things may be heating up. While it is important to read the writing on the walls, it is equally important to cover it over as soon as possible. Don't give the gang a chance to claim your community as their turf by allowing their graffiti to stay intact. Graffiti is an eyesore and decreases the quality of life in a neighborhood. When dealing with graffiti, it is recommended to:

- ✓ **Photograph it (the whole piece and in sections)**
- ✓ **Analyze it while it is intact**
- ✓ **Remove it (paint over it, sandblast it, etc...)**
- ✓ **Keep an archive of the photo**
- ✓ **Document the colors used**
- ✓ **Document the gang 'Tag' names**
- ✓ **Document the indicators of "beef" or violence**
- ✓ **Get involved in, or create, an anti-graffiti program to cover over *all* graffiti. *Get the youth involved!***

How to Identify If
Someone Is in a Gang

Identifying someone as a gang member, today, is not as simple as it may seem. Gang members are much more cautious in displaying their gang affiliation because of the increased attention of law enforcement and scrutiny from communities. Regardless, gang members share similar traits that are hard to cover-up. These traits may manifest themselves in attitude, demeanor, attire, symbols, colors, grooming, and typical gang culture (customs).

Attitude

Many gang members may display an attitude of disinterest in normal social or family functions. Childhood friends may no longer be preferred and replaced by new friends with obvious gang ties. The family will experience his/her disconnection rapidly or gradually. Phrases may be heard like "...*my friends are my family!*" or *"...you don't understand me like they do!"* Truancy may also be occurring.

Demeanor

Gang members tend to act arrogant or aloof. They are preoccupied with fellow gang members and the gang's activities. Gang life can cause them to be unnecessarily paranoid and secretive. Many gang members are involved, in some way, with drugs. This involvement, depending upon the degree, can result in a host of problems and manifestations.

Attire

While gang members, today, are attempting to minimize their overt display of gang affiliation, they maintain an inherent need to **represent** their connection. Many gang members view the total lack of representation as a form of weakness or *'selling out.'* Gang members will create a representation of gang affiliation through discreet signs. These signs could be observed in a pair of shoelaces or baseball hat with a logo or color(s) adopted to represent the gang. Many gangs, today, wear designer clothing chosen for its perceived representation of their gang. Calvin Klein clothing, for example, is preferred by the Bloods gang because the **CK** means *Crip Killer* (to them).

Sports apparel, in which the name has a certain **'gang-created'** meaning, forming a gang acronym, is commonly worn by gangsters. **ADIDAS** athletic wear, for example, means (to the gang) *All Day I Disrespect All Slobs*. Gang members create a variety of acronyms and meanings from sports apparel names to justify wearing the specific clothing line.

Symbols

Gangs are extremely prone to using symbols. They adopt many symbols to represent their gang. Symbols can be hidden on clothing, in jewelry, in tattoos, in graffiti and in writing. Everyday symbols (stars, shamrocks, animals, flags) can be used as well as created (drawn) just for the gang. Gangs will choose clothing and accessories because of the symbols used.

Colors

Color coordinated clothing is common among gang members. Jackets, pants, shirts and dresses (females) in the gang's color, are preferred. Colors can be displayed in accessories, jewelry, or other items worn or carried. The most common way for a gangster to display his/her gang's colors is by wearing a bandana, commonly referred to as a '**flag.**'

Grooming

Some gang members share similar haircuts, hair color, shaving habits, or lack of grooming. Gang members may shave their eyebrows, sideburns or beards in a certain fashion.

Gang Culture (Customs)

Gangs have their own rituals and terminology. It is called **gang culture**. As a person's gang related habits develop, it will be hard for that person to hide his/her affinity for such customs and affiliation to the gang. The gang's customs are usually manifested in the form of their own language, unique hand signs, style of dress, ritualistic greetings, social issues (leadership structure) and symbolism.

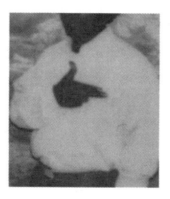

Paying attention to the signs of gangs will enable your ability to recognize if someone is, in fact, in a gang. Paying attention may help to intervene, early, in a person's life before the gang is able to take control.

NOTES

Gangs and Their Symbols

In the following pages, many gang identifiers are shown from gangs affecting North America today. These gangs and other similar groups pose a threat to society and must be monitored closely. It is important to understand the symbols used by these gangs/groups to create a keen awareness of their presence and to educate every citizen to become alert to such gangs/groups.

The following gangs/groups were chosen for their ability to affect most of North America today as well as their ability to recruit in a majority of cities and towns. These gangs/groups are: Bloods. Crips, People Nation, Folk Nation, Latino, Prison, Asian, Outlaw Motorcycle, Hate/Extremist, Occult, Miscellaneous and Terrorist gangs/groups.

Many of the gangs and their symbols can be found throughout the United States, Canada, and other parts of the world, regardless of the region. East Coast, West Coast, Northeast, Southeast, Northwest, Southwest, Midwest or Midsouth, of these United States and Canada, has, in some manner, been affected by the following gangs and groups.

For a brief history and other pertinent information on each of these gangs/groups refer to the Gang/Group Explanation, starting on page 87.

Bloods

Colors: Red, Black, Green & sometimes Brown or Tan

United Blood Nation

3 Burn scars forming, what is called "Dawg Paws"

Piru is the same as 'Blood'

5 Point Star and number 5 signify the Bloods affiliation with People Nation

Paws

Crip Killer

M.O.B.

Member of Blood

Dog Tattoo

Bloods

**Damu' means
Blood in Swahili**

**031 means *'I have
love for you, blood!'***

**East Coast
Bloods hand
sign**

"B.L.O.O.D." sign

Piru Hand sign

B.U.L.L.S.

**Bloods United Live
Longer & Stronger**

Crab
Killa

***Signifies Crip
Killer. Crab is a
derogatory name
for Crips***

Crips

Colors: Blue & sometimes White, Black, Gray or Silver

Crips call each other Cuz (cousin)

Loc

Crips are Loc'd into the gang

Blood Killer

CRIP

Cool
Rule
Important
People

Crip Castle

Skull

Blue boy

Signifies a male Crip member

Signifies blood Killer. Slob is a derogatory name for Bloods

CRIP

Community
Revolution
In
Progress

Crips

**Pitchfork, Heart with Wings, 6 Point Star and number 6
show the Crip's Folk Nation affiliation.**

Crips hand sign   **Harlem Crips**   **Compton Crips**

K.S.W.I.S.S

CCN

Consolidated Crip Nation

•

*Kill Slobs When I
See Slobs*

People Nation

Colors: Black, Gold, Yellow and Red. **Flag to the Left**

Left Pant leg rolled up

5 Point crown

Dress gloves

Top Hat & Cane

5 Point Star

Pyramid with 21 bricks

Champagne Glass

Sword

Crescent Moon

Eye

People Nation

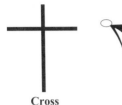

Cross

Playboy Bunny
facing left and/or
left ear bent

All is All   All is Well

Phrases used by People Nation members

People Nation
Crown Hand

People Nation
5 Pt Star Hand sign

Staff

Folk Nation

Colors: Blue, Silver, White and Black. **Flag to the Right**

Heart and wings

Horns

6 Point Star & Pitchforks

Number 6

Right pant leg rolled up

Flame or Torch

Dice with 6 or 3

Heart, Pitchforks, Tail and Horns

Pitchfork

Backwards Swastika

Folk Nation

Sun

All is One

A Phrase used
by Folk nation
members

Bunnyhead
facing right/
right ear bent

Devil's Tail

**Devil and
Pitchfork**

Folk hand sign

Latino Gangs

Hands Praying to God for forgiveness

Netas

Cholo

'M' for Mexican

13 means Sureno   14 means Norteno

Old English Writing & other common Latino Gang sayings:

MI VIDA LOCA!;
My Crazy Life

VATOS LOCOS;
Crazy Homies

PERDONAME MI MADRE
Forgive me Mother

Our Lady of Guadalupe icon

MS - 13

Mara Salvatrucha

Sombrero / Sword

Latino Gangs

Mi Vida Loca

BROWN PRIDE

Means Proud to be Latino

100% Puro

To be 100% Mexican or Latino

Spanish Cross

Latino Criminal Hand Tattoos

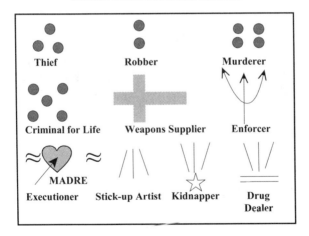

Prison Gangs

Aryan Brotherhood-
"Shamrock"

Nuestra Familia

  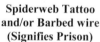

Nuestra Raza

Spiderweb Tattoo
and/or Barbed wire
(Signifies Prison)

Black Guerilla Family

La Eme: Mexican Mafia

Prison Gangs

G25
Group 25

G26
Group 26
Puerto Rico Prison Gangs

G27
Group 27

5%ers Gang

Texas Syndicate

Macheteros

PBB

Prison Brotherhood
of Bikers

B.O.S.
S.O.S.

Brothers of the Struggle
Sisters of the Struggle

Trinitarians
A Dominican Prison gang

Asian Gangs

Serpent

Dragon

Flying Dragon

Ghost Shadows
(Devil's Tail)

Born To Kill
(Coffin)

Panther
(Powerful)

Tiny Rascal Gangsters

Triad Symbol:
Heaven, Earth, Man

Asian Gangs

Asian Boyz

力

STRENGTH

Tiger Tattoo means Power

Tien   **Money**

Tinh   **Love**

Tu   **Prison**

Toi   **Crime**

Thu   **Revenge**

生
喪

BORN TO LOSE

Outlaw Motorcycle Gangs

Dequiallo

"No Mercy"
Ask no Quarter...
Give no Quarter!

MC

Motorcycle Club

FTW

F... The World

22

Been in
Prison

13

Marijuana

1%

1 % er
Outlaw Biker

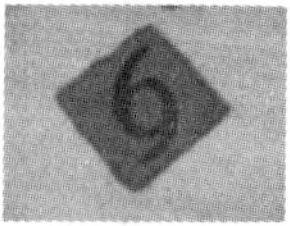

6

Sixty-nine patch

Alphanumerics:

B for Bandidos = 2

O for Outlaws = 15

Filthy Few

P for Pagans = 16

Have killed someone   HA for Hell's Angels = 81

Outlaw Motorcycle Gangs

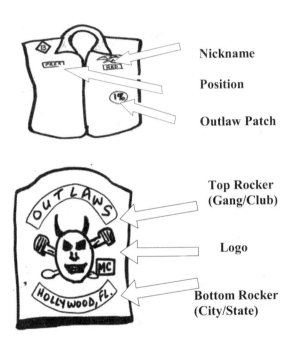

Nickname

Position

Outlaw Patch

Top Rocker
(Gang/Club)

Logo

Bottom Rocker
(City/State)

Hate Groups/Extremists

Lightning Bolt(s) or SS bolts

Iron Cross

Swastika (neo nazi)

Celtc Cross

KKK

Thor's Hammer (Skinhead)

HH means Heil Hilter

88 means HH

420
Hitler's Birthday

Doc Marten Boots

Aryan Brotherhood

Hate Groups/Extremists

World Church
Of the Creator

National Socialist
Movement

National Alliance

Stormfront

Hammerskins

Skinheads

NAAWP

White Aryan
Resistance

Aryan Nation

Occult Groups

Devil Hand Sign

Hexagram

Favored by Satan

Cross of Confusion:
Question Christianity

Satan backwards

**Mark of the
Beast. (FFF=666)**

Ankh

Evil Servant

Evil One

**Where Satan
Appears**

Brimstone

42

Occult Groups

Baphomet

WICKED

Church of Satan

Mouth of the Devil

Cross of Nero

Power Sign

Miscellaneous Gangs

Zulu Nation gang

Together Forever

La Familia

Cash Money Boyz

Latin Kings

INP
International
Posse

Los Solidos

Miscellaneous Gangs

G27

Group 27 Gang
*(A Puerto Rican Prison Gang
turned U.S. Street Gang*

DWB

Dirty White Boyz

Palestine Latino Organization

Straight Edge gang

FTRA

Freight Train Riders of America

Wolf Pack

Goon Stick (FTRA)

Terrorist Groups

Al Jihad

Al Qaeda

Aum Shinrikyo

DFLP

PLO

Sendero Luminoso

Fatah

FARC

Greater Syrian Party

Hamas

Hamas

Terrorist Groups

Hamas Brigades

PFLP

Kahane Chai

Hizballah

MEK

Muslim Brotherhood

PFLP-GC

Palestine
Islamic Jihad

LTTE

PKK

ELN

47

Gang Colors Reference Guide

Gang	*Colors*
20 Luv	Black and Green
Ambrose	Light Blue and Black
Ashland Vikings	Green and Black
Asian Boys	Green, Black and Yellow
Bandidos MC	Red and Yellow
Bishops	Brown and Black
Black Disciples	Black
Black Gangsters	Black and Blue
Black Guerilla Family	Black, Green and Red
Black P Stones (El Rukns)	Green, Black and Red
Black Souls	Black and White
Blood Brothers	Red and Black
Blood Red Dragons	Red
Bloods	Red, Black, Green, Tan
Brotherhood	Black, Silver and White
Brothers of the Struggle	White or Black and White
Brown Pride	Brown
Campbell Boys	Red & Blue; Red & Gold
Cash Money Boys	Green
C-Notes	Green, Red and White
CREAM Team	Red and Black
Crips	Blue
Cullerton Deuces	Gray, Black or White
Deuce Mob	Red and Black
Dominican Power	Red
Dominican Don't Play	Red, White and Blue
Dominos	Black and White
Eighteenth Street	Blue

Gang Colors Reference Guide

Gang	*Colors*
Elm City Boys	Green and Black
Esse	Black, White and Red
Folk	Black, Silver, Blue, White
Fuk Ching	None
Gangster Disciples	Black, Silver, Blue, White
Gaylords	Gray/Black or Light Blue/Black
Gum Sing	None
Haitian Mafia (Crips)	Blue
Harrison Gents	Purple and Black
Hell's Angels MC	Red and White
Imperial Gangsters	Pink and Black
Insane Deuces	Green and Black
Insane Dragons	Maroon and Gray
Insane Unknowns	White and Black
Jamaican Posses	Yellow, Green and Red
Jungle Brothers	Purple and Black
Killer Bees	Red
La Familia (Prison)	Red and White
La Familia (Street)	Red, White, Blue
La Familia Stones	Orange and Black
La Gran Raza (N Y)	Red, White & Green
La Raza (Chicago)	Red, White & Green
Latin Counts	Red and Black
Latin Disciples (Maniac)	Blue and Black
Latin Dragons	White and Black
Latin Eagles	Silver and Black
Latin Gangsta Disciples	Blue and Black
Latin Jivers	Brown and Black

Gang Colors Reference Guide

Gang	*Colors*
Latin Kings	Gold, Black, Red
Latin Locos	Black, White & Brown
Latin Lovers	Red and Yellow
Latin Saints	Blue and Black
Latin Souls	Maroon and Black
Los Papi Chulos	Green and White
Los Solidos	Blue, Red
Mara Salvatrucha (MS13)	Blue and White
Mexican	Red, White and Green
Mexican Mafia	Black
Mickey Cobras	Red, Green and Black
Netas (Asociacion)	White, Black, Red
Netas (Connecticut)	Red, White and Blue
New Breed	Red, White, Blue
Orchestra Albany	Brown and Yellow
Oriental Street Boyz	Blue
Outlaws MC	Black
Pachucos	White and Black
Pagans MC	Red, White and Blue
Party People	White, Black; Maroon, White
People	Black and Gold and Red
PLO	Blue and White
Popes	White, Black; Blue, Black
Purple Philippino Posse	Purple and White
Ruff Ryders	Red
Satan Disciples	Yellow and Black
Simon City Royals	Blue, Black; Blue, Green
Skinheads	Red

Gang Colors Reference Guide

Gang	*Colors*
Solidos	Blue and Red
Spanish Cobras	Green and Black
Spanish Gangster Disciples	Blue and Black
Spanish Lords	Red and Black
T- Street Playaz	Red, Navy Blue and Light Blue
The Hard Pack	Light Blue and White
Tiny Rascal Gangsters	Gray or Blue
Traviesos	Red, White and Green
Two Six Nation	Tan and Black
Two Two Boys	Blue and Black
United Kings	Orange
Untouchables	Black and White
Vagos	Blue
Vice Lords	Gold, Black; Red and Black
Wolf pack	Red
Zulu Nation	Brown, Green, Red

Gang Colors Reverse Reference Guide

Colors	*Gang*
Black	**Black Disciples**
Black	**Mexican Mafia**
Black	**Outlaws MC**
Black and Blue	**Black Gangsters**
Black and Gold and Red	**People**
Black and Green	**20 Luv**
Black and White	**Black Souls**
Black and White	**Dominos**
Black and White	**Neta (NYC)**
Black and White	**Untouchables**
Black, Green and Red	**Black Guerilla Family**
Black, Silver and White	**Brotherhood**
Black, Silver, Blue, White	**Folk**
Black, Silver, Blue, White	**Gangster Disciples**
Black, White and Brown	**Latin Locos**
Black, White and Red	**Esse**
Blue	**Crips**
Blue	**Eighteenth Street**
Blue	**Haitian Mafia (Crips)**
Blue	**Oriental Street Boyz**
Blue	**Vagos (Mexican)**
Blue (light) and Black	**Ambrose**
Blue and Black	**Latin Disciples (Maniac)**

Gang Colors Reverse Reference Guide

Colors	*Gang*
Blue and Black	**Latin Gangsta Disciples**
Blue and Black	**Latin Saints**
Blue and Black	**Spanish Gangster Disciples**
Blue and Black	**Two Two Boys**
Blue and Red	**Solidos**
Blue and White	**Mara Salvatrucha (MS13)**
Blue and White	**PLO**
Blue or Gray	**Tiny Rascal Gangsters**
Blue, Black; Blue, Green	**Simon City Royals**
Blue, Red	**Los Solidos**
Brown	**Brown Pride**
Brown and Black	**Bishops**
Brown and Black	**Latin Jivers**
Brown and Yellow	**Orchestra Albany**
Brown, Green, Red	**Zulu Nation**
Gold, Black, Red	**Latin Kings**
Gold, Black; Red and Black	**Vice Lords**
Gray/Black or Lt Blue/Black	**Gaylords**
Gray, Black or White	**Cullerton Deuces**
Green	**Cash Money Boys**
Green and Black	**Ashland Vikings**
Green and Black	**Elm City Boys**
Green and Black	**Insane Deuces**

Gang Colors Reverse Reference Guide

Colors	*Gang*
Green and Black	**Spanish Cobras**
Green and White	**Los Papi Chulos (Dominican)**
Green, Black and Red	**Black P Stones (El Rukns)**
Green, Black and Yellow	**Asian Boys**
Green, Red and White	**C-Notes**
Light Blue and White	**The Hard Pack**
Maroon and Black	**Latin Souls**
Maroon and Gray	**Insane Dragons**
No colors	**Fuk Ching (Chinese)**
No colors	**Gum Sing (Chinese)**
Orange and Black	**La Familia Stones**
Orange and Purple	**United Kings**
Pink and Black	**Imperial Gangsters**
Purple and Black	**Harrison Gents**
Purple and Black	**Jungle Brothers**
Purple and White	**Purple Philippino Posse**
Red	**Blood Red Dragons**
Red	**Dominican Power**
Red	**Killer Bees**
Red	**Norteno**
Red	**Ruff Ryders**
Red	**Skinheads**
Red	**Wolf pack**

Gang Colors Reverse Reference Guide

Colors	*Gang*
Red and Black	**Blood Brothers**
Red and Black	**CREAM Team**
Red and Black	**Deuce Mob**
Red and Black	**Latin Counts**
Red and Black	**Spanish Lords**
Red and Blue or Red and Gold	**Campbell Boys**
Red over White	**Hell's Angels MC**
Red over Yellow	**Bandidos MC**
Red and Yellow	**Latin Lovers**
Red, Black, Green	**Bloods**
Red, Green and Black	**Mickey Cobras**
Red, Navy Blue and Light Blue	**T- Street Playaz**
Red, White and Blue	**Dominicans Don't Play**
Red, White and Blue	**Netas (Connecticut)**
Red, White and Blue	**New Breed**
Red, White and Blue	**Pagans MC**
Red, White and Green	**La Raza (Chicago)**
Red, White and Green	**Mexican**
Red, White and Green	**Traviesos**
Red, White	**La Familia**
Red, White & Blue	**La Familia**
Red/ White/Green or Blue	**La Gran Raza (New York)**
Red/White/Green or Red	**La Gran Familia**

Gang Colors Reverse Reference Guide

Colors	*Gang*
Red; White	**One Eight Trey (Bloods)**
Silver and Black	**Latin Eagles**
Tan and Black	**Two Six Nation**
White and Black	**Insane Unknowns**
White and Black	**Latin Dragons**
White and Black	**Pachucos**
White or Black and White	**Brothers of the Struggle**
White, Black and Red	**Netas (New York)**
White, Black, Red	**Netas (Puerto Rico)**
White, Black; Blue, Black	**Popes**
White, Black; Maroon, White	**Party People**
Yellow and Black	**Satan Disciples**
Yellow, Green and Red	**Jamaican Posse**

Sports Apparel and Designer Clothing

Sports Team/ Designer	Gang	Symbolic Meaning or Colors/Logo/Acronym
ADIDAS	Crip/Folk	*All Day I Disrespect All Slobs*
All Star (Converse)	Crip/Folk	*All Slobs Turn And Run*
Atlanta Braves	People	"A" for Almighty
Boston Celtics	Spanish Cobras	Green/Black colors
British Knights	Crips	BK for *Blood Killer*
Burger King	Crips	BK for *Blood Killer*
Calvin Klein	Bloods/People	CK for *Crip Killer*
Charlotte Hornets	4 Corner Hustlers Initials	C & H
Charlotte Hornets	Imperial Gangsters	Black/Pink
Chicago Bulls	Vice Lords	Black/Red
	Latin Counts	Black/Red
	Bloods	*Bloods Usually Live Longer Sucka*
	Mickey Cobras/Cobrastones	Black,Red
	Black Peace Stone	*Boy U Look Like Stone*
Chicago Blackhawks	Vice Lords	Black/Red; Star
Converse AllStar	People	Five point star
Dallas Cowboys	People	Five point star

57

Sports Team/ Designer	Gang	Symbolic Meaning or Colors/Logo/Acronym
Denver Broncos	Black Disciples	Switch DB for initials BD
Detroit Lions	Gangster Disciples	Black/Blue
Detroit Tigers	Folk	"D" for Disciples
Detroit Tigers	Gangster Disciples	Black/Blue
DUKE	Folk	Black/Blue
		Disciples Utilizing Knowledge Everyday
		Crown down to Disrespect Latin Kings
Georgetown	Folk	Initial "G" for Gangster
Kansas City Royals	Folk	Black/Blue
Kansas City Royals	Simon City Royals	"Royals"
KSWISS	Crips	*Kill Slobs When I See Slobs*
LA Dodgers	Gangster Disciples	"D" for Disciples
LA Kings	Latin Kings/People	"Kings"
LA Kings	Kings	*Kill Inglewood Nasty Gangsters*
Los Angeles Raiders	Folk	"Raiders" means
		Ruthless Ass Insane Disciples R Shunning It

Sports Team/ Designer	Gang	Symbolic Meaning or Colors/Logo/Acronym
Los Angeles Raiders	People	"Raiders" means
		Raggedy Ass Iced Donuts Everywhere Running Scared
Miami Hurricanes	Insane Vicelords	***May I Admit My Insanity***
Michigan	MLDs	M for Maniac Latin Disciples
Minnesota Twins	MLDs	M for Maniac Latin Disciples
NY Yankees	Gangster Disciples	Black/Blue/White
N. Carolina Tar Heels	Folk	Black/Blue
Nike	Folk	Black/Blue
Nike	Bloods	***Niggas Insane Killin E-Rickets***
Oakland A's	Ambrose	A for Ambrose
Oakland A's	Orchestra Albany	"O" & "A"
Oakland A's	Spanish Cobras	Green
Orlando Magic	Folk	"Magic" means
		Maniacs (MLD) And Gangsters In Chicago
		Black/Blue
Orlando Magic	People	"Magic" means
		Murder All Gangsters In Chicago
Philadelphia Phillies	People/Bloods	"P" for People or Piru

Sports Team/ Designer	Gang	Symbolic Meaning or Colors/Logo/Acronym
San Francisco Giants	Folk	Switch FG for Super Gangster
	Folk	
San Francisco Giants	Future Stones	SF spelled backwards is FS
St. Louis Cardinals	Spanish Vice Lords	Red
Starter Symbol	Folk	Breaking 5 point star logo to disrespect the People Nation
Starter Symbol	People	5 point star
Tampa Bay Lightning	Gangster Disciples	Black/Blue
Texas Rangers	People	T looks like pitchfork going down
University of Illinois	Folk	U & I look like a pitchfork

Symbol/Phrase/Word/# Reference

Symbol/Word/Number	Meaning	Gang/Group
1	*A*	
1%	*1% of Motorcyclists/Outlaws*	Outlaw Motorcycle Gangs
5%	*5 Percenters*	Five Percenters
100%	*Pure of Race*	
150%	*Dedicated to the cause*	Netas
1-8-Trey	*183rd street*	
2	*B*	
2	*B for Bandidos*	Bandidos OMG
2	*Deuce*	Cullerton Deuces
2	*Deuce Mob*	Deuce Mob
3	*C*	
3	*3*	Folk
4	*D*	
5	*E*	
5 words	*I have nothing to say*	White Supremacy, Neo Nazi
5	*5*	All People Nation Gangs
6	*6*	All Folk Nation Gangs
6	*F*	
7	*G*	
7	*G for God*	Five Percenters
7	*Mosque number 7*	Five Percenters
8	*H*	
8TG	*Eight Trey Gangster*	
8T	*Eighty Three*	

Symbol/Word/Number	*Meaning*	Gang/Group
9	*I*	International Posse
10	*J*	
11	*K*	
12	*L*	
13	*M*	
13	*M*	Mexican Mafia, Mexican gangs
13	*Sureno, Sur*	Southern California
13.5	*Judge, Jury & half assed chance*	Outlaw Motorcycle Gangs
14	*Norteno, Norte*	Northern California
14 words	*14 words*	White Supremacists
14	*N*	Northern Structure
15	*O*	
15	*O for Outlaws*	Outlaws OMG
16	*P*	Pagans OMG
17	*Q*	
18	*R*	
19	*S*	
20	*T*	
21	*U*	
22	*Two Two*	Two Two Boys
22	*V*	
22	*Did time in Prison*	OMG
23	*W*	
24	*X*	
25	*Y*	
26	*Z*	
26	*Two Six*	Two Six Boys
31 or 031	*I have love for you, Blood!*	EC Bloods
36 or 036	*Bitch*	EC Bloods

Symbol/Word/Number	Meaning	Gang/Group
74	*Indicates the letters G-D*	Gangster Disciples;FOLK
81	*HA*	Hell's Angels
88	*HH or Heil Hitler*	Neo Nazi, White Supremacy
92	*Nine Deuce; Ninety second street*	
92H	*92 street and Hoover ave*	
125	*Murder (law) in New York*	
187	*Murder (law) in California*	
211	*Robbery (law) in California*	
274	*Indicates the letters B-G-D*	Black Gangster Disciples
347	*Cell phone area code: NY*	
360	*Universal; Complete circle*	People; Latin Kings
415	*San Francisco Area Code*	415 gang
646	*Cell phone area code: NY*	
666	*Anti Christ sign*	Satanic
718	*Brooklyn, Bronx Area Code*	
718	*Queens, Staten Island Area Code*	
777	*AWB founders*	AWB
917	*Cell phone area code: NY*	
1978	*Year Larry Hoover imprisoned*	Folk
16-12	*PL*	Pistoleros Latinos
2 Pitchforks	*Campbell Boys*	Campbell Boys
2 Swastikas	*Supremacy*	Silent Brotherhood
2 & arrow through it	*Insane Deuces*	Insane Deuces

Symbol/Word/Number	Meaning	Gang/Group
3 dots	*Two Sixers*	Two Sixers
3 point crown	*Third World Nation*	Folk
3 Triangles together	*Dirty White Boys*	Dirty White boys
4 dots	*Party dots*	Folk
4 point star	*Black P Stone Rangers*	Black P Stone Rangers
4CH	*Four Corner Hustlers*	4 Corner Hustlers-Vice Lords
5 dots	*Money,Love,Prison,Crime, Revenge*	Vietnamese/Asian gangs
5 dots	*Tien, Thu, Tinh, Toi, Thu+C147*	Vietnamese/Asian gangs
5 point star	*Dianna, the moon goddess*	Satanic
5 seeds	*Seed Brothers*	Mandingo Warriors
A	*Ambrose*	Ambrose
A	*Anarchy*	
A in a circle	*OA*	Orchestra Albany
AB	*Aryan Brotherhood*	Aryan Brotherhood
AB	*Asian Boys*	Asian Boys
ABG	*Any Body Gets it*	Any Body Gets it
ABS (Z)	*Asian Boys*	Asian Boys
ABT	*Aryan Brotherhood of Texas*	Aryan Brotherhood
AC	*Aryan Circle*	A White Supremacist Biker Club
Africa map	*African Heritage*	Zulu Nation
Africa Map in a circle	*Brothers of the Struggle*	Brothers of the Struggle
African shield with 7	*Protection*	Mandingo Warriors
African Warrior	*Overthrow*	415 gang

Symbol/Word/Number	Meaning	Gang/Group
AK 47's crossed	*Resistance*	Aryan Resistance Movement
ALKQN	*Almighty Latin King Queen Nation*	Latin Kings
Allah	*God: Islamic Religion*	Islamic Terrorists; Five Percenters
All is all; All is Well	*A greeting; Everything is OK*	People Nation Gangs
All is one	*A greeting; Everything is OK*	Folk Nation Gnags
AMA	*American MC Association*	Outlaw Motorcycle Gangs
Amer. Flag/13 stars	*Breed MC*	Breed Motorcycle Gang
AN	*Aryan Nation*	Aryan Nation
Anarchy Symbol	*Abolish all laws; Punk*	Satanic/Supremacists/Militias
Ankh	*Egyptian Symbol of Life*	Satanic
Arm holding A hammer	*Skinheads*	Skinheads
AS	*Aryan Sisterhood*	Aryan Nation-Female
Asta la Muerte (hasta)	*Until Death (Hasta La Muerte)*	Prison Gang
Aviator Jacket	*Skinheads*	Skinheads
AW	*Aryan Warriors*	Aryan Warriors
AWB	*Afrikaner Weerstandsbeweging*	Afrikaner Resistance Movement
AWL	*Aryan Women's League*	Aryan Women's League

65

Symbol/Word/Number	Meaning	Gang/Group
Axe	*Supremacy*	
Axe (2 sides) down	*Anti-Justice*	Militias; Satanic
Axes/crossed	*Supremacy*	Neo-nazi
Aztec War Symbol	*Eternal War*	Mexican Mafia; Mexican Gangs
Aztlan	*Aztec homeland*	Mexikanemi
B	*Bishops*	Bishops
B	*Bandidos*	Bandidos MC
Baby G	*Baby Gangster*	
Back Pack	*Full Colors Tattooed on Back*	Outlaw Motorcycle Gangs
Baphomet	*Devil; Black Magic*	Satanic
Barbed Wire	*Over the Border*	Mexican
Barbed Wire/BB	*Border Brothers*	Border Brothers/Mexican
Bat	*Dark religious beliefs*	Goths
BB	*Border Brothers*	Border Brothers/Mexican
BB	*Indicates numbers 2 and 2*	Two Two Boys
BESTLOVE		Eighteenth Street
Better Growth/Development	*Black Gangster Disciple*	Black Gangster Disciples
BF	*Indicates numbers 2 and 6*	Two Six Boys
BFFB	*Bandidos Forever For. Bandidos*	Bandidos MC
Bicycle chain	*Motorcycle gang affiliation*	Outlaw Motorcycle Gangs
Bishop drawing	*Bishops*	Bishops
BK	*Blood Killer*	Crips
Black man w/sunglass.		West Coast Bloods
Black Hand print	*The Black Hand*	La Cosa Nostra

Symbol/Word/Number	Meaning	Gang/Group
Black man w/ ball/chain		West Coast Bloods
Black Panther	*Black Panther Party*	Black Panther Party
Black Rose	*Death; Secret Mission*	Satanic; Latin Kings
Bling Bling	*Sound of Jewelry; Jewelry*	Street Gangs
Blood Droplet	*Shed Blood; Killed someone*	
BNG	*Bahala Na Gang*	Bahala Na Gang
Boricua	*From Puerto Rico*	
Born Fi Dead	*Born to die*	Jamaican Posses
BOS	*Brothers of the Struggle*	Gangster Disciples/ BOS/FOLK
BOS	*Beat On Sight*	
Bow and Arrow	*Hunter*	Santeria
British Flag	*British Hammerskins*	Skinheads
Broom	*Political Ties*	Jamaican Posse
B's Up!	*Bloods Dominance*	Bloods
BTK	*Born To Kill*	Born To Kill
BTM	*Blue Top Mob*	Blood Affiliate gang in NYC
Buddha Symbol	*Buddhist Faith*	Asian Gangs
Bulldog	*Dawg*	East Coast Bloods
Bulldog/gun	*Stop oppression*	Fresno Bulldogs
BULLS	*Bloods United Live Longer Sucka*	Bloods
Bunny head	*Playboy*	
Bunny with Fedora	*Crips*	West Coast Crips
Bunnyhead facing left	*People*	People
Bunnyhead facing right	*Folk*	Folk
	People	People
Bunnyhead left ear bent		
Bunnyhead right ear bent	*Folk*	Folk

67

Symbol/Word/Number	Meaning	Gang/Group
Bui Doi	*Child of the dust*	Vietnamese Gangs
Bunnyhead smoking	*Crips*	West Coast Crips
Buon Phi So Khong	*My life is a zero*	Vietnamese Gangs
C	*Crips*	Crips
Capo	*Mafia Captain; Boss*	La Cosa Nostra
Capo di tutti capi	*Boss of all bosses*	La Cosa Nostra
Caporegime	*Mafia Captain; Boss*	La Cosa Nostra
Cane	*Stylish*	Harrison Gents
Canes crossed	*Harrison Gents*	Harrison Gents
Card depicting '2'	*Deuce*	Deuce Mob; Deuces
Castle	*Crip Castle*	Crips
CB	*Campbell Boys*	Campbell Boys
CB	*Cheap Boys*	Cheap Boys (Asian)
CBC	*Cold Blooded Cambodians*	Cold Blooded Cambodians
CCO	*Consolidated Crip Organization*	West Coast Crips
CD	*Cullerton Deuces*	Cullerton Deuces
Celtic Cross	*White Supremacy*	Aryan Nation
Chain(s)	*Prison*	Prison Gangs
Chalice	*Marielito; Santeria*	Marielito; Occult
Champagne Glass	*Celebration*	People
Champagne glass/top hat	*Vice Lords*	Vice Lords
Ching a ling	*Ching a ling*	Ching-a-ling OMG
Cholo	*Gangster (Spanish)*	Mexican
Cholo with a hat	*Pachuco*	Mexican
Cigarette Burns (3)	*Dog paw*	East Coast Bloods
Circle crossing an A	*OA*	Orchestra Albany
Circle/ 'S' thru a line	*Blessed by Satan*	Satanic
Citizen	*Motorcyclist that is not a 1%*	Outlaw Motorcycle Gangs

Symbol/Word/Number	Meaning	Gang/Group
CK	*Crip Killer/Calvin Klein*	Bloods
Clock with hands	*Time is running out*	Satanic
Clover & three leaves	*Irish Pride*	Aryan Brotherhood
Cobra	*Spanish Cobras*	Spanish Cobras
Cobra	*Mickey Cobras*	Mickey Cobras
Cobra	*King Cobra Boys*	King Cobra Boyz (Asian)
Coffin	*"Until death`*	Born To Kill
Coffin/small cross	*Born To Kill*	Born To Kill
Colt 45 pistol	*Pistol*	Hermandad/ Pistoleros Latinos
Confederate Flag	*White Supremacy; Militia*	
Consigliere	*Counselor*	La Cosa Nostra
Cousin	*Fellow Crip*	*Crips*
CREAM	*Cash Rules Everything Around Me*	Bloods; other gangs
Creativity	*White Supremacy*	World Church of Creator
Crescent moon	*Unity*	People
Crescent Moon	*Mickey Cobras*	Mickey Cobras
Crescent Moon	*Lucifer*	Satanic
Crescent moon & star	*Black P Stone Nation (El Rukns)*	Black P Stone Nation
Crescent Moon and Star	*Islam*	
Crescent moons facing each other	*East and West*	*People*
Cross	*Strength*	People
Cross and dagger	*Latin Lovers*	Latin Lovers

Symbol/Word/Number	*Meaning*	Gang/Group
Cross Branded on one's body	*Natoma Boys*	*Natoma Boys*
Cross of Nero	*Defeating Christianity*	Satanic
Cross on its side	*Weapon Supplier*	Marielito
Cross upside down	*Anti Christ*	Satanic
Cross with a wreath	*Gaylords*	Gaylords
Cross with a dagger through it	*Insane Popes*	*Insane Popes*
Cross with 'LOVE"	*Latin Souls*	Latin Souls
Cross/ rays emerge	*Pachucos*	Pachucos
Cross/religious	*Bishops*	Bishops
Crown with 5 points	*People*	People
Crown/3 point		Dominican or Mexican gangs
Crown/devil's tail/ 'M'	*Texas Mafia*	Texas Mafia
Crown/rounded	*Imperial Gangsters*	Imperial Gangsters
C's UP!	*Crip Dominanace*	Crips
Cuzz; Cuzzin	*Fellow Crip*	Crips
CVL	*Conservative Vice Lords*	Vice Lords
Dai dai lo	*Big boss*	Asian Gangs
Dai lo	*Boss*	Asian Gangs
Dawg	*Dog*	Bloods (East Coast)
DBD	*Death Before Dishonor*	La Cosa Nostra; Outlaw MC
Death head	*Hell's Angels*	Hell's Angels
Dequiallo	*Ask no quarter, give no quarter*	OMG
Devil and Pitchfork	*Satans Disciples*	Satans Disciples
Devil Warrior	*Texas Mafia*	Texas Mafia
Devil's horns	*Campbell Boys*	Campbell Boys
Devils Tail		Folk

Symbol/Word/Number	Meaning	Gang/Group
Dice	*Life is a gamble*	Folk
Dice showing 2	*Deuce*	Insane Deuces; Deuce Mob
Dice showing 2 & 6		Tow Six Boys
Dice showing 3 or 6		Folk
Dice with 2 and 2	*Two Two Boys*	Two Two Boys
Diez y ocho	*Eighteen*	Eighteenth Street
Dip	*PCP*	
Doc Martens (boots)	*Skinheads*	Skinheads
Dog or Dog Paw	*Dog; Dawg*	Bloods EC
Dollar sign	*Money Macks Murder*	C-Notes
Dollar sign	*Cash/ Money*	Cash Money Boys
Dollar sign & 5 pt star	*Vice Lords*	Vice Lords
Dominos	*Latino*	Marielito
Dots/3	*Mi Vida Loca*	Mexican gangs
Double-head Stone Axe	*Chango*	
Dragon	*Courage; Power*	Santeria
Dragon	*Power*	Flying Dragons (Asian)
Dragon in fire	*Latin Dragons*	Latin Dragons
Dragon with a Devilhead		Texas mafia
Dragon in Tower	*Prison Overthrow*	Black Guerilla Family
Dresser	*A fancy Harley Davidson MC*	Outlaw Motorcycle Gangs
DWB	*Dirty White Boys*	Dirty White Boys
Eagle and Snake		Mexican Mafia
Eagle biting Snake	*Mexican*	La Raza-Mid West
Eagle Flying	*Latin Eagles*	Latin Eagles
Eagle flying w/ claws	*Wah Ching*	Wah Ching
Eagle head	*Latin Eagles*	Latin Eagles

71

Symbol/Word/Number	Meaning	Gang/Group
Eagle/intertwined 'N'	Aryan Nation	Aryan Nation
Eagle/sombrero	Revolution	Mexikanemi
ECAB	East Coast Aryan Brotherhood	Aryan Brotherhood
EFCC	Exotic Foreign Cambodian Crips	EFCC
Eightball Patch	Committed homosexual sodomy	Outlaw Motorcycle Gangs
El Rukns	Black P Stone Nation	Black P Stone Nation
Eme	M	Mexican Mafia
EMI	Mexikanemi	Mexikanemi
Ene Efe	NF	Nuestra Familia
Ene Ese	NS	Northern Structure
ER	Extreme Rydas (Riders)	Speed-bike Motorcycle Club
Extreme Rydas	Speed bikers	Motorcycle club/Speed bike trend
Eye		People
Eye with brow	Supremacy	Neo-nazi
Eye with eyelashes	Evil Eye	
F14	Fresno Northern California	Fresno Bulldogs
Face/happy & sad	Comedy/Tragedy; Good/Evil	Solidos Gang
Female face/Swastikas	Aryan Sisterhood	Aryan Sisterhood
FFF	666; Anti Christ Symbol	Satanic
Fist	Black Power	
Five T's	Prison Gang	Asian Gangs
Flame	Arsonist	

Symbol/Word/Number	Meaning	Gang/Group
FUBU	*F--- U Blood Up; (For Us By Us)*	Bloods
G-C-D	*God - Cipher - Divine*	Five Percenters
GL	*Gaylords*	Gaylords
Gloves	*Vice Lords or People Nation*	People
Gloves	*Harrison Gents*	Harrison Gents
Gloves	*Purity*	People
Gloves/palms up	*All is Well*	People
Goat Heads	*Devil*	Satanic
Grimas	*Urine*	Mexican Gangs
Grim Reaper	*Death at your door*	Vampire
Grim Reaper	*Death to your door*	Netas
GSC	*Grape Street Crips*	Grape Street Crips
Halo	*Saints*	Saints
HA; HAMC	*Hells Angels Motorcycle Club*	Hell's Angels Biker gang
Hammer	*Skinhead*	Skinheads
Hammer, Thor's	*Supremacy*	White Supremacist
Hammers crossed	*Skinheads*	Skinheads
Handprint/black	*The Black Hand; Mafia*	La Cosa Nostra; Mexican Mafia
Hands Praying	*Praying to God for Forgiveness*	Latino gangs
Harley Davidson logo	*Associated with Bikers*	
Hat and cane	*Crips*	West Coast Crips
Hat and Cane		People Nation Gangs
Heart	*From the Heart (Corazon)*	Netas
Heart	*Love for Nation*	Folk
Heart with 'madre'	*Executioner; Hitman*	Marielito; Latino

Symbol/Word/Number	Meaning	Gang/Group
Heart with SSS	*Sige-sige*	Sige Gang
Heart with wings	*Spread love*	Folk
Heart with eaglehead & wings	*Latin Lovers*	Latin Lovers
Heart with horns	*Love and Power*	Folk
Heart/Sword through it	*Death before dying*	Folk
Heart/wings	*Spread Love over the Nation*	Folk
Hexagram	*Symbol of Solomon*	Satanic
HH	*Heil Hitler; Supremacy*	Neo-Nazi Movement
HH	*88; Heil Hitler*	Neo-Nazi Movement
Hooded person/ cross	*Popes*	Insane Popes
Horns	*Power to overcome*	Folk
House Mouse	*Girl who hangsaround clubhouse*	Outlaw Bikers
Huelga Bird	*Mexican Power/Pride*	Mexican Gangs
Icon/Christian	*God forgive me*	Mexican
IG	*Imperial Gangsters*	Imperial Gangsters
Imperial Crown	*Imperial Gangsters*	Imperial Gangsters
Imperial Crown & halo	*White supremacy*	Church of the Creator
Infidel	*A Non-believer of Islam*	Used by Islamic Terrorists
INP	*International Posse*	International Posse Gang
Indian Warrior/skull/horns	*Native American Rebel*	Warrior Society
Iron Cross	*White Supremacy*	Outlaw MC Gangs; Supremacists

74

Symbol/Word/Number	*Meaning*	Gang/Group
Iron Cross with a skull	*Motorcycle or Supremacy*	Outlaw MC Gangs; Supremacists
Iron eagle	*Nazi*	Neo-nazi; American Nazi Party
JLP	*Jamaica Liberation Party*	Jamaican Posse
Jump Boots	*Doc Marten Boots*	Skinheads
KCB	*King Cobra Boyz*	King Cobra Boyz (Asian)
King David	*David Barksdale*	Folk nation
Kill ZOG	*Kill Zionist Occupied Government*	Texas Mafia
Knife Dripping Blood	*Kill; Death; Sexual perversion*	Satanic
Knife with 'S' around	*Two Sixers*	Two Sixers
Knight	*Ambrose*	Ambrose
Knight helmet/ spear	*Ambrose*	Ambrose
Knights Helmet w/ LC	*Latin Counts*	Latin Counts
KSWISS	*Kill Slobs When I See Slobs*	Crips
Latin Crown / 5 points	*Latin SupremacyLatin Kings*	Latin Kings
Law Enf. Logo down	*Force against a Law Officer*	Outlaw Motorcycle Gangs
LB	*Lonely Boys*	Lonely Boys (Asian)
LBB	*Long Beach Boys*	Long Beach Boys (Asian)
LBO	*Lonely Boys Only*	Lonely Boys
Lei chi (Lichee)	*Lucky money (extortion)*	Asian Gangs
Lightning bolts	*Supremacy*	Supremacy;Freight Train Riders

Symbol/Word/Number	Meaning	Gang/Group
Lion	*King of the Jungle*	Latin Kings
Little devil	*Satan's Disciples*	Satans Disciples
LJ's	*Latin Jivers*	Latin Jivers
LK	*Latin Kings*	Latin Kings
LKK	*Latin King Killers*	
LLL	*Love, Life, Loyalty*	Black Gangsters
Loc	*Dark Sunglasses; Crip initiation; Crip*	Crips
Long Fingernail	*Drug orientation*	
Lowrider (Low Rider)	*Vehicle customized low to ground*	
LRZ	*La Raza*	La Gran Raza Nation
LS	*Latin Souls*	Latin Souls
M18	*Mexican-Eighteenth Street*	M-18
Machete with a star	*Puerto Rico Revolution*	Macheteros
Machineguns crossed	*Overthrow*	415 gang
Male w/ boots/suspenders	*Skinhead*	Skinheads
Mamas	*Biker whores*	Outlaw Motorcycle Gangs
Maravilla	*Maravilla Housing in Los Angeles*	Maravilla Gang
Mask/African		Zulu Nation
MC	*Mickey Cobras*	Mickey Cobras
MC	*Motorcycle*	Outlaw Motorcycle Gangs
Merlin sketch	*Black disciples*	Black Disciples
Mexican Bandit		New Mexico Syndicate
Mexican Warrior &dagger	*Mexican Revolution*	Mexican Prison Gang

Symbol/Word/Number	Meaning	Gang/Group
Mexicana/Eme	*Mexican Mafia*	Mexican Mafia
Mi Vida loca	*My Crazy Life*	Mexican
Middle finger	*F--- The World*	Outlaw Motorcycle Gangs
Middle finger/ swastika	*Outlaw Bikers*	Outlaws Motor Cycle Gang
MLD	*Maniac Latin Disciples*	Maniac Latin Disciples
MM	*Mexican Mafia*	Mexican Mafia
MMM	*Money Macks Murder*	Folk
MOB	*Money Over Bitches*	
MOB	*Member Of Blood;*	Bloods
Monk	*Simon City Royals*	Simon City Royals
Monk/hood over face	*Insane Deuces*	Insane Popes/Unknowns
Moon (1/3) with a face	*Mickey Cobras*	Mickey Cobras
Moon/crescent	*See crescent moon*	
Mouthpiece	*Mob Lawyer*	
MPR	*Money Power Respect*	General; Bloods
MS13	*Mara Salvatrucha-13*	Mara Salvatrucha
Mud People	*Derogatory name for Minorities*	White Supemacicts
Mustache/goatee	*Cholo Symbol; Mexican Gangster*	Mexican Gangs
Mutilated Animals	*Satan Worship*	Satanic
My Life is a Zero	*I have no future*	Vietnamese/Asian gangs
NATAS	*Satan spelled backwards*	Satanic
Nazi Helmet	*Supremacy*	Neo-Nazis
NEMA	*Amen spelled backwards*	Satanic
NF	*Nuestra Familia*	Nuestra Familia

Symbol/Word/Number	Meaning	Gang/Group
NIKE	*Niggas Insane Killin Ericketts*	Bloods
NLR	*Nazi Low Riders*	Nazi Low Riders
NMS	*New Mexico Syndicate*	New Mexico Syndicate
Nomad	*No specific chapter*	Outlaw Motorcycle gangs
NS	*Northern Structure*	Northern Structure
NTG	*Nine Trey gangsters*	East Coast Bloods
OG	*Original(ating Gangster)*	
OK	*Oriental Killers*	Oriental Killers
Old Lady	*Bikers girlfriend or wife*	Outlaw Motorcycle Gangs
OOO	*Triple O (Original Gangster)*	East Coast Bloods
OPM	*Other Peoples Money*	
OPP	*Other People's Property*	
P and a cross	*Pachucos*	Pachucos
Pachuco	*Gangster*	Mexican
Pakhan	*Godfather; Don*	Russian Mafia
Palm Tree	*Religious; Puerto Rico*	Santeria; Netas
Panther	*Power to overcome*	Black Panthers; BTK
PBB	*Prison Brotherhood of Bikers*	Prison Gang
Peace Sign		Zulu Nation
Pee Wee	*A young gang recruit (pre-teen)*	
Pentagram	*Spirit, wind, fire, earth, water*	Occult
Pink Panther	*Imperial Gangsters*	Imperial Gangsters

Symbol/Word/Number	*Meaning*	Gang/Group
Pitchfork	*Struggle*	Folk
Pitchfork/downward	*Disrespecting Folk Nation*	People
Pitufo	*Smurf*	Mexican Gang
Playboy Bunny	*Vice Lords*	Vice Lords
PNP	*People's National Party*	Jamaican Posse
POBOB	*Pissed Off Bastards Of Bloomington*	Hell's Angels
PoPo	*Police*	
PP	*Party People*	Party People
Property of	*Belonging to a Biker*	Outlaw Motorcycle Gangs
Prospect	*Biker recruit*	Outlaw Motorcycle Gangs
PRS	*Puerto Rican Stones*	PR Stones
P.R. Flag with 2 stars	*Puerto Rican Revolution*	FALN
Puppy	*Gun*	Jamaican Posse
Pyramid	*Strength*	People
Pyramid	*Black P Stone Rangers*	Black P Stone Rangers
Pyramid	*PR Stones*	PR Stones
Pyramid and a star	*Black P Stone Rangers*	Black P Stone Rangers
Pyramid with 21 bricks	*People*	People
Pyramid with and eye	*People Nation*	People
Question Mark	*The Deadly Ones*	The Deadly Ones
Question Mark	*Bahala Na Gang*	Bahala Na Gang
Question mark/ down	*Questioning Christianity*	Satanic
	Crips	West Coast Crips
Quill Pen and Paper		
Rabbit	*Latin Eagles*	Latin Eagles
Red Laces	*Skinheads*	Skinheads

79

Symbol/Word/Number	Meaning	Gang/Group
Red Suspenders	*Skinheads*	Skinheads
Redrum	*Murder spelled backwards*	Satanic
Rifle	*United Vice Lords*	Vice Lords
Rottweiler	*A symbol of power*	Gangster Disciples
R's	*Royals*	Simon City Royals
RTC	*Rollin Thirties Crips*	Crips
Run	*Sanctioned biker outing*	Outlaw Motorcycle Gangs
RZ	*Raza Loca or Crazy Females*	(La) Raza Loca; Mexican females
S sideways	*Brothers of the Struggle*	Brothers of the Struggle
Sailing ship in full mast	*Hung Pho Gang*	Hung Pho Gang
Saint drawing	*Saints*	Saints
Saint stick figure & cane	*Saints*	Saints
SB	*Seed Brothers*	Mandingo Warriors
SC	*Spanish Cobras*	Spanish Cobras
Serpent		Satanic
SGDN	*Spanish Gangste Disciple Nation*	Spanish Gangsters
Shaolin	*Staten Island*	Wu tang
Sheep	*Biker whores*	Outlaw Motorcycle Gangs
Shield with A's	*Ambrose*	Ambrose
Skull & crossed pistons	*Outlaws Logo*	Outlaws Motorcycle Gang
Sige- Sige	*Sige*	Sige Gang (Pacific Islands)
Skull		Prison; Outlaw MC Gangs; Crips
Skull behind bars	*Prison*	Prison Gang

Symbol/Word/Number	Meaning	Gang/Group
Skull Tattoo	*Crypt keeper*	Crips
Skull with Swastika	*Deadmen MC*	Deadmen Motorcycle Gang
Skull with Viking horns	*Motorcycle or Supremacy*	Outlaw MC Gangs or Supremacists
Skull/batwings	*Mexican Mafia logo*	Mexican Mafia
Skull/fangs	*Revolution*	Arizona Mexican Mafia
Skull/rose	*Prison gang*	Mexican Mafia
Skull/wings on the head	*Motorcycle affiliation*	Outlaw Motorcycle Gangs
SL	*Spanish Lords*	Spanish Lords
SMG	*Silver Middle Gang*	Silver Middle Gang
SMM	*Sex Money Murder*	Bloods
Snake		Satanic
Snake with 7 heads	*Revolution*	Symbionese Liberation Army
Snake with an X across it	*Abaqua Cult Symbol*	Abaqua Cult
Snake around a T	*TS*	Texas Syndicate
SNM	*Sindicato Nuevo Mexico*	New Mexico Syndicate
Sombrero/dagger	*Revolution*	Nuestra Familia
SOS	*Sisters of the Struggle*	Sisters of the Struggle
SOS	*Shoot On Sight*	
SOS	*Sons Of Silence*	Sons Of Silence OMG
Spade	*Cullerton Deuces*	Cullerton Deuces
Spade with 2 & two dots	*Cullerton Deuces*	Cullerton Deuces
Spanish Cross	*Spanish Gangsters*	Spanish Gangsters
Spears crossed	*Protection*	Mandingo Warriors

Symbol/Word/Number	Meaning	Gang/Group
Spiderweb	Stuck in a web; Prison	Prison Gangs
Squares (Two)	Supernatural Power	Satanic
SS	Nazi	Neo Nazi Movements
Staff/3 prong	Third World Nation	Folk
Staffs crossed	Power	People
Star (5 pt)/three lines	Kidnapper	Marielito; Latino gangs
Star David X'd out	Anti Semitism	Neo Nazi Movements
Star/5 pointed	Respect,Honesty,Unity,Knowledge,Love	People Nation Gangs
Star/5 Point Broken	Disrespect toward People Nation	Folk Nation Gangs
Star/6 pointed	Star of David	Folk
Star/6 Pointed Broken	Disrespect toward Folk Nation	People Nation Gangs
Star/8 pointed		Five Percenters
Star: 5 Pointed	Puerto Rico	Netas; La Familia
Star: 5 Pointed	North Star	Norteno gangs
Sunglasses/dark	Loc's	Crips
Sunglasses/dark	Knowledge	Folk
Sur (eno)	Southern California	Latino Gangs
Swastika	Neo-nazism	Skinheads; White Supremacists
Swastika and a D	Latin Disciples	Latin Disciples
Swastika backwards	Maniac Latin Disciples	Maniac Latin Disciples
Swastika/lightning	Nazi	American Nazi Party

Symbol/Word/Number	*Meaning*	Gang/Group
Swastika/shield & sword	*Overthrow*	Aryan Brotherhood Texas
Sword	*Overthrow*	Aryan Brotherhood Texas
Sword in a fire	*Wrath of Allah*	People
Sword/rifle	*Revolution*	Black Guerilla Family
S X E	*Revolution*	Straight Edge
T Ese		Texas Syndicate
T w/ black circle around it	*The Order*	The Order
Tail of Devil	*Devil's follower*	Satanic
Talisman	*Satanic beliefs*	Satanic
Target sight	*Shoot; kill; mark for death*	
Tax	*Street tax; Tribute; Surcharge*	
TDO	*The Deadly Ones*	The Deadly Ones
Teardrop-closed (dark)	*Shed blood; Killed someone*	
Teardrop-open (outline)	*Shed tear for a fallen comrade*	
Tiger	*Power*	Multiple Gang Uses
TM	*Texas mafia*	Texas Mafia
Top hat	*Gentlemen*	Harrison Gents
Top Hat	*Classy*	People
Top hat/cane/gloves	*Classy*	Vice Lords
Torch	*Overcome*	Folk
TOS	*Terminate On Sight*	
Tower/prison	*Prison*	Black Guerilla Family
TP or TTP	*Treetop Piru*	Bloods (West Coast)

Symbol/Word/Number	Meaning	Gang/Group
Trece	*Spanish word for 13*	Mexican: Latino
TRG	*Tiny Rascal Gang(sters)*	An Asian street gang
Triangle	*Where demon appears in rituals*	Satanic
TVS	*Traviesos (Misfits)*	Traviesos Gang; Mexican
TS or ST	*Syndicato Tejano*	Texas Syndicate
UK	*Unknowns*	United Kings (Crips)
UK	*United Kings*	Insane Unknowns
UBN	*United Blood Nation*	Bloods
UCVL	*United Concerned Voters League*	Unknown Conservative Vicelords
UK	*United Kings*	United Kings (Crips)
Umoja	*Mandingo Warriors*	Mandingo Warriors
Universal	*Full Circle; Meeting*	Latin Kings; People
Viking head	*Supremacy*	White Supremacists
Viking Helmet	*Supremacy*	Aryan Warriors
Viking silhouette	*Ashland Vikings*	Ashland Vikings
VL	*Vice Lords*	Vice Lords
Vor	*Thief (gangster)*	Russian Mafia
Vory v Zakone	*Thieves in law (gangsters)*	Russian Mafia
Waldas	*Bahala Na Gang*	Bahala Na Gang
WAR	*White Aryan Resistance*	White Aryan Resitance
War shield w/ 2 feathers	*Native American Warriors*	Warrior Society; Native American
Watermelon		Mandingo Warriors

Symbol/Word/Number	*Meaning*	Gang/Group
Watermelon/5 seeds		Mandingo Warriors
WAU	*Women for Aryan Unity*	Aryan Nation
White Cross		Outlaw Motorcycle Gangs
Wet	*PCP*	Crips
What time is it?	*You are going to die!*	
White hood	*White Supremacy*	KKK
White Cross	*I stole something from a corpse*	Outlaw Motorcycle Gangs
Wings		OMG
Wolf	*Derogatory name for Police*	Russian Mafia
Woodpecker	*Knights of the KKK*	Peckerwood; White Supremacy
X w/circles each end	*Evil Servant*	Satanic
X w/small x's & o's	*Abaqua Cult Symbol*	Abaqua Cult
XII	*12; L*	
XIII	*13; M; Southern California*	Sureno; Mexican; MS13
XIII	*13; M; Southern California*	Norteno: Mexican
XIII	*13; MS-13*	Mara Salvatrucha
XIV	*14: N; Northern California*	Norteno; Mexican
XVIII	*18; Eighteen*	Eighteenth Street
XXX	*Straight and Narrow*	Straight Edge
Yellow Jackets	*Black and Gold*	Latin Kings
YG	*Young Gangster*	
Yin Yang	*Good/Evil; Black/White; Night/Day*	

Symbol/Word/Number	Meaning	Gang/Group
YLO	Young Latino Organization-MLD	Latin Disciples
You Feel It		Kents
You know what time it is?	You are going to die!	
Zionist	Jew	
Zoot Suiter	Pachuco/gangster	Mexican gangs
Zoot Suiter	Gangster; Pachuco	Pagans OMG
Zutar	Pagans Logo	Pagans OMG

Gang / Group Information

BLOODS

    Bloods gangs can be found in many of the fifty states. They have their strongest presence in California where they originated in the early 1970's and in New York where they were founded in 1993. Bloods advocate a new unity of all Bloods gangs called 'United Blood Nation'. Bloods call each other Dawgs and are mortal enemies of the Crips, thus, they will cross out the letter 'C.'

CRIPS

Crips were formed in Los Angeles, California during the late 1960's. They can be found in most of the fifty states. They formed on the East Coast during the early 1990's and are enemies with the Bloods. Their color is Blue. They cross out the letter "B". Crips, because of their affiliation, will use many of the Folk Nation Symbols.

PEOPLE NATION

The **People Nation** coalition was formed in the Illinois Prison System during the 1980's as a 'gang alliance'. People Nation gangs, today, are Bishops, Bloods, Cullerton Deuces, La Familia Stones, Insane Deuces, Kents, Latin Saints, Latin Kings, PR Stones, Black P Stones, Popes, Latin Counts, Mickey Cobras, Spanish Lords, Gaylord, Insane Unknowns, Pachucos and Vice Lords. People Nation considers Folk Nation gangs their enemies. People Nation gangs will use the left side as their representative side. Hats, etc., will be tilted to the left. The number 5 is the number that represents them.

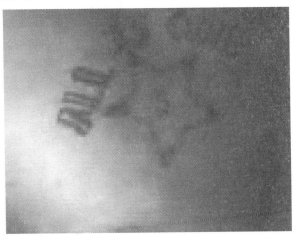

FOLK NATION

The Folk Nation coalition was formed in the Illinois Prisons in the 1980's as a gang alliance. The following gangs, are members of the Folk Nation: Ambrose, Black Gangster Disciples, Harrison Gents, La Raza, Latin Eagles, Latin Souls, Satan's Disciples, Spanish Gangsters, Ashland Vikings, Crips, International Posse, C-Notes, Imperial Gangsters, Maniac Latin Disciples, Latin Jivers, Orchestra Albany, Simon City Royals, Two Two Boys, Two Sixers, Black Disciples, New Breed, Campbell Boys, Popes, Latin Dragons, Latin Lovers, Party People and Spanish Cobras. Folk Nation gangs consider People Nation gangs their enemies. Folk Nation gangs use the number 6 and will use the right side as their dominant side.

LATINO GANGS

Latino gangs have formed among many Latin cultures. The largest gangs are 18th Street, Mara Salvatrucha (MS13), Netas, Dominicans Don't Play, Latin Kings, La Raza, Surenos and Nortenos. Many of these gangs share symbols and phrases. Most of the 50 states have Latino Gangs and apparently, those Latino gangs of Mexican nationality are rapidly growing throughout the US and Canada.

PRISON GANGS

Prison gangs are often affiliated with gangs on the 'outside'. Many times, they are a reflection of the local community gangs in which they are located. Prison gang affiliation consists mainly along ethnic, racial, religious, and political lines. Prison gangs, such as the Aryan Brotherhood and Nazi Low Riders are also racist in nature.

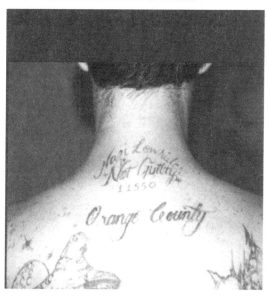

ASIAN GANGS

Traditionally, most Asian gangs avoided flaunting their gang membership. Outward display by dress or graffiti was scarce among these Asian gangs. The older, more traditional gangs are Flying Dragons, Ghost Shadows, Korean Power, Born To Kill, Gum Sing, Fuk Ching, and Ghost Shadows. There are, however, several growing Asian gangs across the United States taking on a typical American gang style and flaunting their membership. Some of these gangs are Asian Boyz, Wah Ching, Tiny Rascal Gangsters, Cambodian Crips, Filipino Bloods, Bahalana Gang and several others.

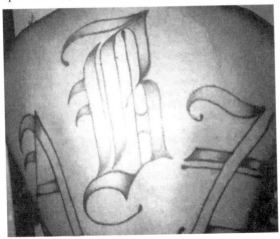

神 GOD

災 EVIL

強 BRAVE

工 SKILL

切 EXTREME

驚 AMAZING

平 和 WORLD PEACE

平 SIMPLE

名 WISE

小 PRETTY

特 SPECIAL

約 PROMISE

信 TRUST

目 ATTRACTIVE

組 UNITE

連 TOGETHER

奇 STRANGE

良い GOOD

悪い BAD

熱い HOT

野 WILD

94

OUTLAW MOTORCYCLE GANGS

Outlaw Motorcycle Gangs are prevalent across the country and in many countries outside the United States. The American Motorcycle Association estimates 99% of all Motorcycle riders are legitimate people. The remaining 1% are Outlaws (1%ers). The Major Outlaw Motorcycle Gangs (1%ers) are Hell's Angels, Outlaws, Bandidos and Pagans. Some other Outlaw Motorcycle Gangs are Sons of Silence, Rock Machine which has patched over to Bandidos, Breed, Warlocks, Avengers, Iron Horsemen, Ghetto Riders, Ching A Lings, Sixty Niners, Renegades, and many others.

HATE GROUPS/EXTREMISTS

There are many Hate Groups in America today. Previously listed are just some of the symbols of some of these groups. Many groups hide their true identity by calling themselves Religious or Political Groups. The main hate Groups in America are Skinheads (Racist), Christian Identity Groups, KKK, Black Separatists, White Supremacists and Neo-Nazis.

OCCULT GROUPS

Occultism is widespread through the United States. Many of our young people are experimenting in occult rituals. Although Satanic practices are not illegal, we should be aware of their signs and symbols, especially since some individuals involved in such practices have committed illegal acts and use the cover of Satan Worship to commit crimes and sexual assaults.

MISCELLANEOUS GANGS

The gangs and symbols depicted in the Miscellaneous Gangs section consist of those gangs that either do not fit into another category or need to be singled out for their influence on society. Such gangs, like the Latin Kings, Los Solidos, Zulu Nation (Northeast US), International Posse (So. Florida) and others have proven to be extremely violent, exist for many years despite law enforcement prosecutions, and remain involved in the drug trade.

TERRORIST GROUPS

Unfortunately, there are far too many Terrorist Groups threatening our world today. September 11th, 2001 has shown us how devastating the death and destruction from terrorism can be. While the Terrorist Group symbols are a representation of their affiliation, we must be aware that many of these terrorist groups hide under a blanket of religion and tend to represent a distorted view of their respective religion. We must not, although there are similarities in symbolism and culture, assume that a varied use of the depicted terrorist symbols is, in fact, a terrorist. We should, however, be aware of their presence in our society and report any suspicious activity indicating terrorism or any sightings of the specific logos to law enforcement.

Disclaimer

While all of these symbols, colors, numbers, logos. acronyms, and words have been used by the gangs or groups mentioned in this Pocketguide, the authors of this book, by no means, imply everyone using these symbols, colors, numbers, logos, acronyms, and words are affiliated with such gangs/groups.

At no time does the author imply every gang/group mentioned in this Pocketguide, with like or similar names, is involved in criminal activity. And the author does not imply that every associate of the gang/group mentioned is a criminal.

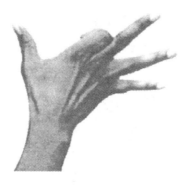

Other Pocketguides by Lou Savelli available from Looseleaf Law Publications

Basic Crime Scene Investigation

Proactive Guide for Law Enforcement for the War on Terror

Identity Theft, Understanding and Investigation

Graffiti

Spanish for Law Enforcement Officers

Street Drugs

Cop Jokes

(800) 647-5547   www.LooseleafLaw.com

Homefront Protective Group's Newest Law Enforcement Training Programs

- **Street Cop Tactics™**
- **Counter Terrorism for Local Law Enforcement**
- **Identity Theft: Interdiction and Investigation**
- **Crime Fighting Strategies**

For information on our Co-hosting Seminars contact us:

Toll Free: 877-232-7500
E-mail: homefrontprotect@aol.com
Website: www.homefrontprotect.com